Greaseless:

How to Thrive without Bribes in Developing Countries

Grease·le$$

How to Thrive without Bribes in Developing Countries

Loretta Graziano Breuning, Ph.D.

System | Integrity

PRESS

www.SystemIntegrityPress.com

Published in the United States by System Integrity Press
Copyright © 2004 by Loretta Breuning
Oakland, California
All Rights Reserved

Illustrations by William M. Sharp
Design by Kay Holmes, Design Guidance

ISBN # 0-9744642-0-1

Library of Congress Control Number: 2003096296

System | Integrity

PRESS

www.SystemIntegrityPress.com

Acknowledgments

For all the students who have honored me with their stories.

For everyone who respects the rules without waiting for others to do it first.

For all the friends who have kept my blood circulating when I would have stayed at my desk writing.

And for my creative and witty family, Bill, Lauren, Kyle and Peter.

"All change begins . . . with our choice of intent: the intent to protect or the intent to learn . . . to protect and avoid, or to learn and take responsibility."

"At any given moment we are either protecting or learning."

"When we're closed and protected, we discount, deny or simply refuse to hear new information."

"It is only through the intent to learn that a person can . . . examine false beliefs. There are two conditions necessary . . . (1) belief in good reasons, and (2) willingness to experience pain."

Margaret Paul
Inner Bonding

Contents

Foreword

Corruption is a ubiquitous phenomenon, but anyone raised in a developing country (India for me) will testify that it's particularly onerous. It pervades every aspect of common citizens' daily life. The causes are debatable, but the effects are clear—dysfunction of public agencies, decaying of public infrastructure, and ultimately, scant respect for and adherence to any common civil code of good citizenship. Nor does the effect stop at public agencies. Corruption leads to inefficiency and lost productivity in the private sector, creating a suboptimal climate for investment, both domestic and foreign. The huge economic loss due to bribery and corruption is documented by a large and growing body of research, reported by organizations such as the World Bank, Transparency International, and the Center for International Private Enterprise.

Managers from developed countries face a huge dilemma. They lack the experience to deal with endemic corruption and bribery on a mass scale. And they are bound by laws that classify bribery in foreign countries as a crime.

For these reasons, a practical "how-to" book for managers is much needed—a book that does not tell them to look the other way, or do as the Romans, or naïvely impose Western style beliefs and practices. Nothing else in the managerial literature details operational strategies for functioning in countries where bribery and corruption are common parts of business culture. This book fills the need for strategic guidance on how to deal effectively with corrupt officials and employees and build within them the idea that it is not in your and THEIR best interest to expect "business as usual" from you.

I think you will find this book an effective guide towards precisely that objective. In following the advice given in this book, industries from developed countries can impart to the developing world not just jobs and material wealth, but also a work culture based on accountability and trust, which ought to be the most vital of foundation of all commerce. I believe that two generations need to be raised with the rule of law before it truly takes hold in a nation's culture. This book is a guide for that journey.

Dr. Joyendu Bhadury
Chair, Dept. of Management and Finance
California State University, Hayward

1 Why Even Talk About This?

a. Dirt swept under the rug is still there.

b. Corruption is a matter life and death.

c. Integrity brings prosperity

My story

I was a United Nations Volunteer in the 1970s, assigned to the Ministry of Planning in a central African country. Our team of economists was there to prepare national income statistics, charting the country's flow of earnings and expenditure. The country got much of its income from foreign aid, so it was reasonable for the international community to expect an accounting. Yet the leader of the country refused to release any data. As far as he was concerned, the money was his, and it was no one else's business what he put into one pocket or took out of the other. You could keep your job at the Ministry of Planning if you accepted this premise, but you would not have any work to do. Over a dozen international and local economists, desks piled with paper, had nothing to do because everything was a secret.

To fill in the time, I decided to study Spanish. I took lessons from a neighbor, a high-ranking UN administrator's wife. During my Spanish lessons, I heard the frustration of this administrator because his organization's medical supplies were disappearing. It seems the country's own Minister of Health was having shipments of donated medicine diverted at the port in a neighboring country, and sold for his own account. My teacher told me that her husband could do nothing about it. "Everyone already knows," she explained. "If he publicly embarrasses the government, he'll be fired. And he'll have trouble getting another assignment. They'll say he doesn't get along with people. We have a child now." Her story meshed with what I already learned at the Ministry of Planning.

a. Dirt swept under the rug is still there

"We don't think of it as corruption," one often hears. "It's just the way things are done here."

What you call it is irrelevant. Diverting public resources for private use is corruption. Violating the public trust—like bribing an inspector to certify a building that doesn't meet safety codes—is corrupt, whether you call it that or not. Paying a kickback to a public official in order to make a sale violates the public's trust in that procurement official. And since the cost of the kickback is built into the purchase price, public funds are diverted for private gain.

People learn to live with corruption the way they live with cockroaches. Look the other way when the lights go on so the vermin have time to reach their hiding places. Ignore how disgusted you feel. Forget they're crawling everywhere when you're not looking. If have you always lived with corruption, you could feel disgusted without consciously noticing.

Corruption is like the proverbial elephant in the room. ("I don't see an elephant.") People can negotiate business standing next to an elephant without letting on that it's there. If the elephant smashes furniture, they don't see that either. "It's not my fault," everyone reasons. "It was already there when I came in."

Ignoring corruption means ignoring the damage it does. Our purpose here is not to condemn corruption on moral grounds, but to understand the damage it does.

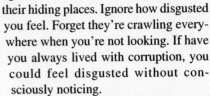

Corruption is like having an elephant in the room. Everyone pretends not to notice, even when the elephant smashes furniture.

b. Corruption is a matter of life and death

Corruption is a leading cause of human suffering. Funds destined for famine relief and water purification disappear into secret bank accounts. Bribes provoke lapses in the regulation of hazardous materials, airport security, food safety, and road safety. Corruption makes it impossible to sustain the infrastructure required by a modern economy (electricity, telecommunication, transportation). In the end, it raises prices and lowers service for everyone.

Individual acts of corruption seem trivial, but the consequences reverberate. When funds for repairing an electricity plant disappear, power outages result, which scares away investors who would have created jobs. When pothole-repair funds disappear, roads become impassable, so farmers can't sell their crops. When medicine disappears, children die of preventable illnesses, motivating families to have more babies than they can nourish and educate.

Some abuses are very big, while others are very small. Big corruption makes headlines, but small corruption is so pervasive that it adds up to large amounts. Arguments about who is more guilty are a waste of time because they do not plug the leaks. If a Minister of Health steals a big chunk of a hospital's budget, and the nurses steal medicine from the hospital stockroom to sell privately, the useful question is not "who is worse?," but "how much medicine gets to the public?"

If your job is to sell medicine to this hospital, you may find yourself face-to-face with corruption. You can go along with it, and become a thread in the fabric of corruption. Or you can resist, and help unravel that fabric. Each person who reads this book can pick at one thread of the fabric until it disintegrates.

The goal is not to destroy something but to create something. An honest system must replace the corrupt system. Weaving a fabric of integrity is more important than catching corruption.

c. Integrity brings prosperity

Not everyone is corrupt. People who say everyone is corrupt obscure the huge difference between systems that are basically functioning and systems that aren't. You experience a system with integrity every time you go to a public restroom and find toilet paper available for your use. Toilet paper is there because funds budgeted for that purpose were actually spent on it, and everyone in the chain of restocking the bathroom honored their assigned task.

If you live in the world where bathrooms supply free toilet paper, you take system integrity for granted. You don't marvel at it every time you use the facilities. On the contrary, the smallest failure in the system provokes great agitation. The famous failures of American electricity unleash huge agitation, and the problem are soon solved. Solving problems is the mark of system integrity. In some countries, blackouts are routine for years and nothing changes.

In most of the world, there is no free toilet paper. Once you leave the "free" world, you have to bring your own. The system does not provide basic amenities, so you don't expect it. This is often blamed on poverty. But in a sense, it's the cause of poverty. When everyone has to provide their own drinking water, it costs more than a municipal water system with integrity. When each business has to generate its own electricity, it costs more. When goods have to be air-freighted because roads and ports don't work, everything costs more, so everyone is poorer. The cost in time and effort is at least as burdensome as the money cost.

System integrity brings prosperity because everyone gets more value out of the resources that are available. A road has more

Infrastructure depends on bureaucracy to channel money from users and taxpayers to equipment and maintenance crews.

value when drivers stay in lanes. In countries where people do not drive in lanes, they get less road capacity for their money. Where road-repair budgets are diverted into private pockets, potholes soon grow out of control. In many countries, roads are so overburdened that trucks average less than twenty miles an hour. Everything costs more because transportation between buyers and sellers is so limited.

If you live in a country where disease is spread by untreated sewage, you would rather have a new public sewage system than a new pair of jeans. You would gladly contribute your fair share of a public wastewater management system. But that option only exists if there's a system for collecting small contributions and ensuring they get directed to the infrastructure. Without such a fabric of integrity, you have to settle for the jeans.

People who live with system integrity don't notice it. If you live in a world where cars drive in lanes, you might get angry at small infringements of your lane without noticing the system's success at channeling volume. If you live in a world with modern banking, you might complain for months about one discrepancy in your bank statement without noticing that billions of transactions are successfully processed each day. In some countries, banks run out of money and just shut down and you lose everything. In some countries, each deposit or withdrawal involves long waits in sweaty mobs at multiple counters staffed by indifferent clerks with pencils and ledger books. The quality of life rests on the integrity of these support systems, but we don't notice it the way a fish doesn't notice water.

Corruption is a substantial violation of public office for personal gain.

☑ Just because you disagree with a public official doesn't mean they're corrupt; reasonable people differ on the best allocation of resources.

☑ There's nothing wrong with personal gain unless it's achieved by diverting public wealth.

☑ Gifts are only corrupt if they induce a public official to violate their responsibility.

We refuse to be courted by gentlemen whose wealth comes from corruption.

2 How Do I Know If a Bribe is Expected?

a. Don't confuse disorganization with corruption.

b. Expectations vary from person to person, even day to day.

c. Make sure your foreign partners aren't "taking care of things" for you.

My story

I got shaken down at the Miami airport and didn't realize it until years later. My little girl and I were at the Mexicana Airlines counter on our way to climb the Yucatan pyramids. The ticket agent refused to check us in because minor children need consent from both parents to enter Mexico. Since my husband was not with us, I needed a notarized permission letter from him. It was 7 a.m., and we had been up all night en route from San Francisco to Miami.

The rule is reasonable, since custody battles have spilled across borders. But there is no system for communicating the rule to ticket buyers before they show up at counters with their sleep-deprived children a continent away from the missing parent. Where did that leave me? Our friendly Mexicana ticket agent had an idea. "Write a letter saying you're divorced with full custody, and have it notarized."

And where would I find someone to notarize this lie in an airport at 7 a.m.? The ticket agent called over an assistant. "There's a notary in the basement, isn't there? Maybe he's open. Escort these ladies down there."

The reader will have no trouble guessing that there was no notary down there, open or shut. It was my only hope of getting on the flight, though, so I scoured that basement with my exhausted child. Our escort seemed to be following more than leading.

I'd lost track of time when I heard him speaking into his walkie-talkie in Spanish. He turned to us and said, "Run!"

"What?"

"The flight is leaving in one minute. They're holding the gate for you. Run!"

That's the whole story. I know nothing more. Years later, when Transparency International caught my attention and I started talking with my International MBA students about corruption, I remembered the experience with new perspective. The pieces fit. The ticket agents realized I would let the plane leave without me before I would slap them some cash. Maybe they took pity on my child (for having such an inept mother?). So they let us go.

The option of slapping them some cash had never occurred to me, in fact—not at the ticket counter, not in the basement, and not when we arrived in Mexico to face a whole new round of formalities.

If it had, would I have had the courage to keep my wallet shut until the last minute? I'm not sure. Being savvy about corruption is not necessarily the best way to work.

Make every good faith effort to comply with legitimate public functions before concluding there is more than meets the eye.

a. Don't confuse disorganization with corruption

Corruption rarely takes the form of a direct demand to which you could "just say no." More often, you have a vague sense of being stuck, and appeals to the rules don't get you unstuck. Some readers will think this is obvious. Others will think, "this doesn't happened to me."

In a corrupt environment, there are no firm rules. When you ask for the rules, no one seems to know. In truth, they may not know, because no one has played by the rules in so long, or even asked. If the rules are written somewhere, they're so vague that they amount to the whim of the official. Anyway, complying with the rules entitles you to nothing, because the official has the power to block you until you motivate him to step out of the way. Or not. Perhaps things are just slow. Perhaps things are working according to the rules, but not at the speed you are used to. Time is precious when you're working with another country—straining with telecommunications, or living in a hotel. When things don't move, you want to know why, fast. But there may be no fast answer. Perhaps the official in charge has not even decided yet how he is going to process you. Perhaps he wants more time to size you up before he decides what the "rules" are.

You should take more time to size him up. Do not assume everything is spelled out in some rulebook. Whether you are clearing Customs or presenting an engineering proposal to the Ministry of Public Works, tune in to the individual. This does not mean to ignore the rules and comply with his personal whim. Just pause for an information-gathering step. Act cooperatively, listen for cues, and after you understand what is expected you can define the ways in which you will and will not cooperate. Don't make assumptions; each interaction is unique.

Say for example you're exporting medicine to a country called Kleptopia. You get a large order from a Kleptopian pharmacy, and now you need permits from Kleptopia's drug regulators and import authorities. These government routines are necessary to protect consumer safety and collect taxes. You must comply even if the process is inefficient.

A dishonest process is different from a disorganized process. Regulators have a legitimate interest in data on the purity of your medicine; but requests for data can also be a move in a game in which the quality of your product is irrelevant to whether or not it passes "inspection." Every time you comply with a rule, another rule might pop up. Similarly, trade officials decide what tax rate to applies to your medical imports. Yet tax and trade rules can become bargaining chips that serve no purpose other than to extract your "cooperation" with a scheme that diverts funds from Kleptopia's public treasury. It is *not* suggested here that all regulatory processes are corrupt and shortcuts are in order. You must make every good faith effort to comply with legitimate public functions before concluding that there is more than meets the eye.

Sometimes you do not find out about corruption until it is too late. A corrupt judiciary is a prime example. Once a judge makes a ruling, it's too late for you to learn about the process behind it. Judges take bribes in many countries, and the other party in the dispute is likely to know this. The Old Testament of the Bible says it's a sin to bribe a judge if you committed a crime. Left unsaid is the ancient belief that if you didn't commit the crime, of course you have to bribe the judge. Bidding wars for the judge's favor are always a risk. Corrupt judges are politically protected, and their loyalty to their political backers will come before all other considerations, including yours.

The difference between disorganization and corruption may be so fine that only insiders can interpret each step of the process. Often you are expected to engage a professional insider for hire. Do not rush to this conclusion, however. You may get the system to work with integrity if you give it enough time and attention.

b. Corruption varies from person to person, even day to day

If your medicine has to jump through ten hoops in Kleptopia, five hoops might have a real public purpose, and five hoops might exist only as entrepreneurial ventures for bureaucrats with positioning power. Of the five legitimate regulations, some may be administered with an honest process and some may not be. It depends whose desk your file landed on. Or which day. An administrator who honors the organization one day may honor his pocket the next day. It could depend on his bills, his risk assessment, or his expectations about you.

Ideally, one wants to know the rules in advance. If your product's lab tests don't really interest them, you'd rather know before you have the tests done. But your friendly government regulator may not have a fixed methodology. He may be looking for feedback from you. How much of a hurry are you in? How hungry are you for this business? He may assume you prefer grease payments over paperwork unless you let him know otherwise. Maybe so few customers select Plan A that he forgets to offer it.

Pay attention to the regulator's area of expertise. The more he knows about the details of the matter, the more likely he's a respecter of system integrity than a gatekeeper who achieved his position some other way. When the person holding up your paper-work expresses an interest in "friendship," it can be a sign that he will not play by the rules. But it can also be taken at face value. He is saying, "I am here for opportunity as much as you are." Find opportunities for him that do not abuse the public trust.

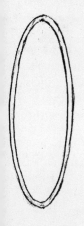

As soon as you comply with one rule, another might pop up. If you grease your way through, you reward obstruction instead of production.

c. Make sure your foreign partners aren't "taking care of things" for you

When you search for foreign partners, you may be referred to individuals with personal ties to government powers. You may even be steered toward the person that everyone knows is the conduit between a certain government official and his Swiss bank account. The people steering you may assume that's what you were looking for—the front-person to whom the cash is paid. If you transact with that person, the courts can make the case that you had "reason to know" you were participating in corruption. Know your foreign agents and partners well; do not settle for their assurances that you just relax and leave everything to them.

The Foreign Corrupt Practices Act of 1977 holds American managers responsible for bribes paid on their behalf by foreign partners. Saying you didn't know does not absolve you if the court holds you had "reason to know." Purposeful ignorance will not keep you out of trouble. You are responsible for finding out what your partners and associates are doing, and you had better pursue the facts with the same rigor that would prevail in court.

The law only prohibits bribes to win business. It does not pertain to routine bureaucratic services like permits and inspections. It *does* cover sales to every sort of government entity—for example, the sale of pharmaceuticals to Kleptopian government hospitals, its military and government-owned companies. If your Kleptopian agent won such sales with corrupt payments, you could be in trouble even if you didn't know about it.

Your foreign partner knows how to blend corrupt payments seamlessly with the culture. For example, exchanging holiday gifts is a widespread tradition, but gifts with huge monetary value can compensate public officials for past or expected future favors. In China, red envelopes filled with money are routinely given and received at the new year. The red envelopes are tiny. "How much money could you possibly fit in them?" I asked a Chinese colleague. "Checks and plastic cash or debit cards go in them these days," he explained. The public official will wait until the holiday season for his bribe if there are long term bonds of trust between him and your foreign partner. It's corrupt if he is violating the public trust to do a favor for your partner. If you are awarded a sales contract by that official, and your firm is the ultimate source of the money in the envelope, then you too are guilty of a corrupt practice.

Knowledge must be pieced together from many different sources. Check Transparency International's Corruption Perception Index, and search TI's huge resources and links (*www.transparency.org*). Background on a country's business climate is available from the U.S. Dept. of Commerce's site, *www.export.gov*. Many consulting and law firms provide more specialized data at a cost.

Generate information from your foreign partners by asking detailed questions, and don't accept vague answers. Insist on being informed of their marketing and lobbying strategies, particularly when sales to the government are involved. By law, you must expressly forbid your overseas representatives to make corrupt payments to public officials on your behalf. You must take the initiative to train and monitor them, and you must be able to show evidence of these initiatives.

Develop alternative sources of in-country information so that you really understand the local operating environment and government procurement practices. When you visit, talk to banks and other service providers, and a variety of investors, multinational and local. You will gather enough pieces to figure out how things are done.

The Foreign Corrupt Practices Act of 1977:

☑ outlaws bribes to get business from public officials, including any employee of a state-owned enterprise

☑ punishes payments made by third parties on your behalf unless you have evidence that it was done against your firm policy

☑ excludes "grease" payments for routine services when accounted for with proper controls and disclosures

The Automatic
Bribe-refusing Machine

Stops corruption instantly with the flick of a switch.

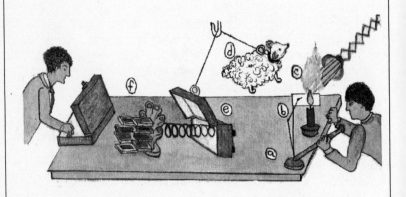

1. Gentleman marshals willpower and integrity to pull lever (a)
2. which strikes flint and creates spark that lights candle (b).
3. Flame burns Swiss bank account documents (c).
4. Sheep (d) notices loss of Swiss bank account and goes searching for greener pastures,
5. pulling chain that releases door of safety deposit box (e),
6. which releases spring-action anti-corruption mechanism (f). Patented process works every time.

3 Don't I Have to Respect Their Culture?

No. Corruption is not their culture.

Yes. You must understand cultures that value personal loyalty more than institutional responsibility.

Maybe. Respect parts of the culturethat don't violate system integrity.

My story

I landed in Moscow at midnight and lined up for a baggage cart. The line was long because people bring lots of imports and winter clothes into Russia. The supply was short—exactly zero luggage carts on hand for the hundreds of disembarking passengers. Occasionally, a porter slowly wheeled up a few carts and headed back out to round up more. As I waited in line, I noticed passengers with big fur hats handing cash to the uniformed employee at the head of the line. I saw the employee raise his hand and push the cash away. Then he pointed to the end of the line. He was operating a system with integrity in the face of temptation and pressure.

No. Corruption is not their culture.

If a foreign buyer asks you to demonstrate your friendship by making a deposit into his secret offshore bank account, its secrecy is proof he knows he's violating a norm. If his culture condoned this behavior, he'd do it out in the open.

Sometimes it *is* virtually out in the open. Singapore is now a success story of the worldwide anti-corruption movement, but in the 1960s, Singapore customs agents could be seen leaving work with full shopping bags in each hand—the day's catch of liquor, cigarettes, and other gifts from travelers anxious to clear customs easily.

Transparency International is a non-governmental organization (NGO) leading the worldwide fight against corruption. "Transparency" means things are done in the open according to established rules rather than by some hidden process. The philosophy of Transparency International is that no culture condones corruption. Every culture in the world distinguishes public resources from private resources.

Every culture has a sense that stealing from the public is wrong; yet some cultures accept this wrong as understandable, something to be expected. Adultery and alcoholism have been viewed that way in some cultures. Humans do many things that are not condoned by their cultures (domestic violence, gambling, predatory competition). Sometimes an unaccepted behavior is only winked at rather than condemned as shameful. In much of the world, corruption is only winked at.

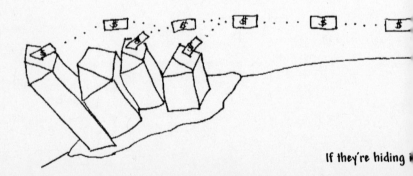

If they're hiding ⬤

Yes. You must understand cultures that value personal loyalty more than institutional responsibility.

Unquestioning loyalty to superiors is the highest value in many cultures. Personal allegiance equals morality. Abiding by the written rules of formal institutions is not a priority in some countries. Organizations lack power. Only individuals have power. Honoring those individuals is what matters, whether or not it conflicts with the rules of an organization.

In short, the rules are whatever powerful individuals say they are. The powerful are not expected to confine themselves to an explicit, fixed set of rules. They are expected to pursue their self-interest, and share the rewards. Loyal subordinates get protection and a cut of the rewards. Conflicts are typically resolved through personal power struggles without reference to written rules.

In traditional cultures, you have unlimited obligation to people with whom you have existing ties, and zero obligation to people with whom you have no personal ties. Your cousins and nephews have a claim on your paycheck; but people you don't know have no right to your consideration, even at work.

During my time in the foreign aid establishment, I heard of a village where people chopped wood from a bridge to use as firewood. Aid donors built the bridge so the people could get crops to market towns. Why would they undermine their economy for firewood? Poverty is not a good enough

they know it's wrong, so it's not really "the culture."

explanation. This kind of self-dealing clearly *causes* poverty. Perhaps people thought the wood was there for the taking—"if I don't take it, someone else will." In some villages, a local chief asserts personal control over a bridge, for his own gain. This seems to solve the problem. People are clear about their personal obligation to the chief, and stay away from the wood. There may be no habit of feeling responsible for something impersonal like a bridge, even though its value is obvious.

Self-dealing has many popular explanations. An official who skims money from a project budget is said to be helping his family or his ethnic group. Fantasies of Robin Hood robbing from the rich to give to the poor lend honor to theft. Stealing from an organization or institution is easier to explain away when the culture does not honor such abstractions the way it honors personal power.

Personalized morality makes it difficult to sustain a modern organization. Most comforts of modern life rest on bureaucracies—people organized around a set of rules to achieve a purpose. The word "bureaucracy" has gotten a bad image, so we overlook the benefits of large-scale organization in our lives: infrastructure works, costs in time and money are kept down, and rules are applied evenly. People who find fault with bureaucracy underestimate the task of getting a huge asset to work (a port, an oil refinery) without losing money.

A bureaucracy has to generate money to pay everyone's salary. Individuals earn their salary by accomplishing tasks that generate money. To do this, they must temporarily put the institutional needs above their personal needs. Even one's superior is bound by the rules of the organization; you are not responsible to his personal needs, but to the organizational needs he represents. Of course there are exceptions, but in the long run, the organization would die if its purpose were ignored.

In some countries, there are buildings full of salaried staff with no purpose that generates resources. The individuals are not responsible for tasks; they are only responsible to the person with the power to get them a seat in a building that pays salaries. No one is concerned about undermining the system; it seems like amassing power to get seats in a free-money building *is* the system.

People may not feel that their salary obligates them to any particular work. Everything one does on the job is a "favor" to someone. A waiter may not feel obligated to serve people who sit down in his restaurant. A ticket seller may not feel obliged to sell seats to just anyone who walks up to his ticket window. A janitor may not feel obliged to unlock a door just because he is keeper of the keys. His power over the keys is precious and is not squandered lightly. Someone who wants service is asking for a favor, period.

Where does the money come from to keep a system like this going? No one asks themselves that question. The organization is treated like a goose laying golden eggs, not as an operation whose budget will be cut unless it provides satisfactory service to clients. Will the enterprise go out of existence if expenses exceed revenues? Will taxpayers and voters withdraw support for the non-performing organization? Will professional reputations be undermined? No. Life feels secure as long as one remains in good standing with one's benefactor. Personal relationships seem real; formal appropriations seem illusory. Whether the golden goose lives or dies is not your business. That's a matter for more powerful people who would probably punish you for interfering.

Deeper cultural motivations are not changed by writing peoples' names on an organization chart. If things only get done through personal ties, a stranger will not perform a service for you just because he has the title and the salary. If you're unfortunate enough to have no personal ties, you have to create them.

He has a right to his culture. You have a right to build your bridge somewhere else.

People may imagine their employer is a golden goose, and collect their golden eggs without caring if the goose is fed.

Maybe. Respect parts of the culture that don't violate system integrity.

When you approach a government official in a traditional society, consider his perspective. You expect a favor from him, but he does not owe you a favor. He's expected to share his wealth with so many; yet you have more wealth and don't expect to share it with him.

Obligation works both ways in his world. If his nephew needs a job, he is obligated to help find one. But then the nephew is obligated to him for any favors that can be done on the new job. There's nothing dishonorable about expecting special treatment from your nephew while he's on the job, even if he has to break the rules of his organization. You are honorable because you helped your nephew when he needed it.

People keep a detailed accounting of favors given and received. A favor received today may have been earned by great effort in the past, sometimes going back generations. People who lack a history of mutual obligation may try to create it with cash. Cash is a fast way to build personal obligation. If you're tempted to do that, ask yourself why you're trying to go so fast? Because your culture is time-pressured. You are respecting your culture, not his.

Your business partner sees himself as an ethical person because he honors his personal obligations. You do not want to suggest that he is unethical. But you want him to process you without violating the public trust. Explain that this is your ethics. Ask that your ethics be respected while you respect his. Search together for a personalized exchange of favors that does not violate the public trust.

Your foreign partner could think:

☑ My salary doesn't obligate me; everything I do is a favor.

☑ I don't owe you a favor; I already owe so much to others.

☑ Whether the Golden Goose lives or dies is not my responsibility, or even my prerogative.

4 What harm does it do, anyway?

a. Corruption erodes the infrastructure.

b. Corruption threatens economic competitiveness and public health and safety.

c. Corruption undermines accountability and trust.

My story

When I was in Moscow, I wanted to buy a ticket to the Bolshoi Ballet. I heard there were two options: an expensive package tour from a travel agency, or bargaining with scalpers on the steps of the theatre. Isn't there a box office, where you just walk up and buy a ticket? No, said my informant. (This was 1993.)

I do not like to bargain, so I devised a clever strategy. I arranged to meet an elderly Russian lady on the steps of the Bolshoi to deliver a letter I had hand-carried for her. I did not know her, but this was a common friend-of-friend, word-of-mouth solution to the unreliability of the Russian Post Office. I assumed she would show her gratitude by bargaining for me. She never showed up, so I was left to fend for myself. Fearing demands for $50, I approached a scalper with the line: "I only have $5. Do you have any $5 tickets?" He said yes, and I congratulated myself for my brilliance. When he left, I saw the price printed on the ticket. It was the Russian-ruble equivalent of seventy cents.

Clearly, the money generated by the Bolshoi ballet was being diverted into scalpers' pockets rather than funding the upkeep of this priceless architectural heritage. Maintenance money would have to come from the depleted Russian Treasury. Otherwise, the building would decay (a disaster for Russian tourism), or be privatized.

a. Corruption erodes the infrastructure

Modern systems require enormous support. Once a water or power system is built, it needs continual repair and replacement to stay in service. Transportation and communication systems need massive organizational effort to keep going. Money must be collected from users of a service and distributed to workers who operate and repair it. Spare parts must be ordered, paid for, distributed and installed. If the maintenance budget was already spent creating desk jobs for everyone's relatives, the system falters.

While infrastructure is expensive, it's easier to solve the money problem than the organization problem. Money is available from international institutions because infrastructure is the foundation of economic progress. But when organization fails, infrastructure fails. When maintenance is neglected, ports slow, buses stall, water purification plants pump impure water. This makes it harder to collect user fees, which makes it harder to fund maintenance. Electricity and telecommunications projects often experience a vicious cycle. User fees aren't collected with integrity, so maintenance suffers. Maintenance funds aren't managed with integrity, so service suffers, therefore users don't pay, and the cycle continues.

Infrastructure tales get complicated. In Equatorial Guinea an electric power plant was built by the foreign aid program of China. The Guinean government agreed to operate and maintain the plant after an initial training period. It did not honor the agreement and the plant was often out of service, leaving the capital city without electricity. The Chinese decided to just run the plant themselves. They even paid for imported petroleum to fuel the generators, and for maintenance crews brought in from China. The outcome was surprising. The Guinean government imposed a high import tax on the petroleum—essentially taxing China's donation. And the Guinean government refused to repair the road leading to the power plant. The road was so strewn with potholes that the Chinese maintenance trucks needed frequent replacement. China pleaded with the Guinean officials responsible for these impasses, and finally just walked away from the project. Huge expenditures are tragically wasted when there is no fabric of integrity to protect them.

Infrastructure investments need a culture that protects them technically and financially. People are welcome to have any culture they want; but if their culture diverts resources from planned purposes, they may find themselves without functioning water, electricity and transportation.

b. Corruption threatens economic competitiveness and public health and safety

"What harm is a gift to someone who earns so little?" one often hears.

Gifts do lots of harm if they reward workers for violating their responsibility. Small acts of negligence add up to huge damage when multiplied by a huge number of workers.

In some places, truckers expect to pay bribes to pass safety inspections. They do not expect their brakes to actually be inspected. A trucker who needs brakes may tell himself it can wait until next week, or the week after. If brake failure causes an accident, he can bribe his way out of any penalties.

In some countries, builders fear their construction projects will be stopped unless they bribe building inspectors. They do not expect the cement they pour to actually be inspected. They may start with good intentions, but when time and money run low, they cut corners dangerously. In an earthquake, buildings made of low-quality concrete crumble instantly.

Food safety inspectors and hazardous waste inspectors may accept gifts that seem small compared to the GDP. But the impact is obviously huge.

Imagine a responsible executive passing through Customs. "I'll just give a little gift to avoid a time-wasting scene," he may think. "I'm no drug smuggler." But once "gift-giving" becomes a habit, he realizes how easy it would be to exceed his allowable limit of alcohol and electronics without paying the huge import tax. It's easy to justify one little decision, and then another. The importance of import taxes may not be obvious. Import tax was the sole source of revenue for the United States government in Washington for the first fifty years of its existence. No import taxes, no government.

Corruption discourages investment because it increases risk. Citizens of corrupt countries often send their savings out of the country to invest. They understand the risk of leaving fixed assets near regulators who can make any demands they want. Investing is left to foreigners and to the handful of citizens with power to work the system to their advantage. Foreigners underestimate risk because they don't understand the arbitrary power of public officials.

Businesses in corrupt environments have higher costs and lower productivity due to the burden of arbitrary regulation and dysfunctional infrastructure. The result is fewer jobs and lower pay. The lower pay does not offset the inconvenience of doing business in that environment, leaving the country with few prospects of creating jobs outside the golden-goose sector.

c. Corruption undermines accountability and trust

It's hard to maintain a functioning system if people believe they can violate rules with impunity. A library is a simple example. If everyone respects the rules, the library has the book you need when you need it. If you lose a book, you pay to replace it. When your book is overdue, you pay a fine. These penalties might annoy you if rule enforcement is not your custom. Perhaps you would rather bring the librarian gifts instead of honoring the rules. You could tell yourself that friendship is more important than rules. You could convince yourself that the librarian made a mistake. Or that she will pocket the money. Or that you don't lose nearly as many books as other people.

But a "friendly" and "flexible" librarian inevitably results in books disappearing. The more the books are missing, the more people convince themselves that "everyone does it" when it's not convenient for them to return a book. The easier it is to ignore the rules of the library, the easier it becomes to ignore the rules of other public institutions.

No one likes to have rules enforced on them. But if you spend time in a rule-observing environment, you learn that rules support services that benefit you. You accept the rules because they apply to everyone. Once you're in the habit of expecting accountability, severe enforcement methods are not necessary. When there is no expectation of consistent enforcement, people may feel entitled to benefit from a system without respecting the rules that preserve its existence.

A system without accountability poses a difficult choice. You can obey the rules and shoulder the burden for people who don't. Or you can violate the rules and participate in the eventual collapse of the system. Shouldering the burden for others harms your pocketbook today. Participating in corruption harms others in the future. Corruption thrives because the consequences are displaced onto others in the future.

The dynamics of accountability are evident in the tax collection process. Tax collection agents in some countries take bribes in exchange for cutting people's tax bills. Citizens feel justified because the tax codes are vague and extreme. (They say that if you paid all the taxes imposed, you would owe more than you earned). Some tax agents take the initiative to extort bribes by threatening to raise a citizen's tax bill. Sometimes they have false receipts printed, to divert funds without the taxpayer's knowledge. These actions deprive the government treasury of funds needed to operate basic public services. Governments respond by raising tax rates, which increases tax fraud. Governments that can't collect taxes tend to default on their debt, which undermines the country's whole banking system.

Corrupt systems do not necessarily involve money. Schools are corrupt if teachers give students points they didn't earn. This robs students who earned the points honestly by lowering the value of the degree. It robs taxpayers who fund education that isn't educating. Academic corruption is theft even without cash changing hands.

Wasted time is a significant feature of corrupt systems. Consider an airline that gives your seat away to someone who pays a last-minute bribe. Over time, you have no reason to make reservations if you do not believe it will hold your seat. People have good reason to bribe if they assume everyone else in the plane or train or theatre got their seat that way. Corruption feels more efficient than wasting time in the waiting room. But in the long run, a system without reservations wastes time and money because it cannot run at peak efficiency. A system without reservations fluctuates between over-utilization (which increases the total amount of waiting time) and under-utilization (which wastes the value of expensive equipment).

Every country has its own form of accountability and trust. In many cultures, networks of personal relationships act as rule-enforcement systems in everyday life. But if a country wants a modern standard of living, it needs accountability and trust in the technical and legal systems that support productivity.

What's wrong with saying "everybody does it"?

☑ Your transportation, sanitation, and communication systems would not exist if everyone broke rules with impunity.

☑ Cynicism does not make you sophisticated; it's a convenient way to justify your own dishonesty.

☑ If you don't know, ask your mother. (Go ahead. Put the book down and call her, now.)

5 Everybody Does It; Why Put Myself at a Disadvantage?

a. Not everyone is doing it.

b. Bribery is illegal and punishable worldwide.

c. Corruption can hurt earnings;
   integrity can help earnings.

d. Because it's not you.

My story

Mexico had high import barriers before NAFTA, as many developing countries did. Mexico protected its auto industry by banning imported cars. Entrepreneurs smuggled U.S. cars into Mexico. One year, the Mexican government announced an amnesty program, waiving penalties on illegally imported cars if people would register them. Some of the eligible cars were owned by U.S. retirees living in Mexico. I visited one of these retirement communities and heard that people had paid US$600 to a local entrepreneur for the service of having their car walked through the auto registration process. It seems the gentleman left town with the cash, ostensibly for government offices in the capital, and never returned. The local newspaper conducted an investigation and determined that the individual had no official authority, and indeed the government had not even established procedures for the amnesty program yet. The purported service was a fraud and the money was never recovered.

Uncertainty in a government's regulatory process attracts entrepreneurs who offer expediting services. Are they selling their time and knowledge? Or corrupt influence? Or nothing? Research is essential.

a. Not everyone is doing it

The earnings of state-owned oil companies have a way of disappearing. One of the many leakages occurs while gas is being transported. Drivers of state-owned gasoline tankers pull over to the side of the road and sell gas directly to passing motorists. When they finally reach gas stations for official deliveries, their tanks are quite low. Shortages result in long lines at the gas stations. This increases drivers' incentive to flag down petrol trucks on the road, and buy from them directly.

Routine annoyances like this create the impression that "everyone is doing it." Yet there are truck drivers who don't, and workers in every sort of job who don't. Efforts have been made to quantify the percentages of workers who do and don't in various countries and occupations. (Search the Transparency International website for research studies.) The people who don't are as hard to count as the people who do, so you tend to see what you want to see.

> The people who don't are as hard to count as the people who do, so you tend to see what you want to see.

Some people use small crimes to justify big crimes. A manager who steals money from the company sees workers taking paperclips and says "everybody's doing it." But everyone knows that's not the same.

Some people overestimate corruption to explain their own limitations. A company could lose a sale because it didn't meet real customer needs, and blame corruption instead. A business might lose money because it's disorganized, and blame corruption. It's hard to get enough information to determine the truth. Researching the underlying details is so challenging that it's tempting to say "everyone's doing it."

b. Bribery is illegal and punishable worldwide

The United States was the first country to punish citizens for participating in *other* countries' corruption. An American manager who bribes a foreign official to win business risks substantial fines and imprisonment. A European manager, until recently, could openly deduct foreign bribes as a tax expense. New regulations prohibiting extraterratorial corruption have been adopted by most countries and international organizations. The new rules will be difficult to enforce, but at least the path has been carved. (Corruption inside a country's own borders has always been officially illegal.)

Corruption charges are hard to prosecute, so the laws are written carefully. They focus on large-scale corruption to win business rather than "grease" payments for routine services. The U.S. Foreign Corrupt Practices Act of 1977 only restricts bribes to "public officials," which includes employees of state-owned enterprises, such as airlines, telecommunications and petroleum companies. Expediting payments for routine services are permitted, but the Act requires full disclosure of them in financial statements.

The law holds Americans responsible for the actions of their foreign agents and partners. American managers cannot just look the other way while the dirty work is done. They must actively enforce anti-corruption policies through training and audited internal controls. One can imagine strategies for circumventing these rules, but the risks motivate American managers to take them seriously. The risks include personal fines, exclusion from U.S. government contracts, criminal penalties, and embarrassing publicity worldwide.

Similar rules have been adopted by the European Union, the International Chamber of Commerce, the World Trade Organization, the United Nations, the Global Coalition for Africa, the Organization of American States (Latin America), and APEC (Asia Pacific Economic Cooperation). Extraterritorial regulation exists because local anti-corruption laws may not be enforced. However, some corruption cases do emerge from a host country's courts and newspapers. Political rivalry rather than routine enforcement tends to motivate the process. Nevertheless, unsavory relationships can percolate from local politics to global headlines.

Skill at working with integrity creates competitive advantage with respect to these laws. A firm that knows how to accommodate corruption but not how to resist it is less flexible, a competitive disadvantage.

c. Corruption can hurt earnings; integrity can help earnings

Lawful contracts are not protected by the courts in many countries. Doing things the legal way would thus appear to have no benefit. When the high road seems blocked, the low road is tempting. But the low road has just as many obstacles. Corruption can cost more than you expected when you took the first step. Once you part with your cash, there is no way to ensure that envisioned privileges materialize. Movies and novels glorify "honor among thieves." In real life, it's risky to do business with corrupt individuals. There's no recourse if a corrupt agreement is violated. That's why violence is the enforcement mechanism of organized crime.

Unsavory relationships can percolate from local politics to global headlines.

Many different things can go wrong. The individual who sells you his influence may ultimately lack the power to deliver the privileges he promised. You might have to purchase influence over a second individual or organization. There could be a bitter power struggle over your friendship that drags your firm's name into the press. You could be expected to bid for influence against competitors, raising the cost to a level you would have rejected if you knew from the start. As soon as you get past one dishonest gatekeeper, another may appear. New demands can appear after you have poured millions of dollars worth of concrete. In the end, it could be faster and cheaper to make it clear from the start that you will refuse all demands. If your rival gets the business, you could be better off!

d. Because it's not you

Diverting public resources to private use is not your way. Maybe you can get away with it, but it's still not you. You can beat your kids with impunity in some places; yet you don't consider doing it when you go there.

You have no right to engage in another country's corruption because you will not be there to live with the consequences. Local citizens can choose corruption if they want to because they have to live with it.

A guilty conscience is not worth the price. The sheer anxiety of getting caught is as significant as the moral drawbacks. I spent a week in Ghana worrying about tiny black-market currency exchanges. Machine-gun-toting border guards were the Ghanaian government's method of enforce an extremely artificial exchange rate. Proof of legal currency exchange was required as you left the country to discourage black market trades. But the official exchange rate was so extortionary that people told me "don't worry, everybody does it." Fear and dread of the exit process ruined my trip, and I would leave an opportunity to my competitor before I would accept such a choice again.

Good reasons to resist:

- ☑ corrupt agreements are not enforceable and can lead to repeated extortionary demands

- ☑ entanglement in local politics risks embarrassing headlines

- ☑ accounting irregularities can devastate stock prices

- ☑ a worldwide consensus on extra-territorial anti-corruption law is emerging

- ☑ avoid criminal and civil penalties for violating the U.S. FCPA

- ☑ peace of mind from contributing to system integrity

6 How Else Can I Get Anything Done?

a. Build non-cash relationships.
b. Communicate system integrity in detail.
c. Negotiate

My story

I once discussed these facts of life with a group of women from India. "Bribery is unnecessary in India," one of them insisted. "My family never pays." The others were incredulous. She explained: "when my mother needs a train ticket, she chooses the ticket window staffed by a person from her native village. She chats with him about local news and gossip (with a long line behind her), and he sells her the ticket without getting a 'tip'." Her mother likewise invites the postman for tea and cookies instead of paying cash. Yet the system has its limits. The woman explained that she needed documents from an Indian library in the course of writing her Ph.D. dissertation. The librarian refused to retrieve the documents without a tip. So the woman just accepted that she would do without that data. Her family builds non-cash goodwill or they do without.

a. Build non-cash relationships

In a market economy, business is an impersonal transaction. I have tomatoes. You need tomatoes. We both benefit. It's nothing personal.

In other cultures, everything is personal. Nothing is just business. Proposing even a simple transaction without acknowledging the other person's humanity is offensive. You pretend to be motivated by the pleasure of their company, and keep your goal-oriented thoughts to yourself.

Personalizing business is an efficient way to get things done if you are born into a large network of influential people. Otherwise, it can be pretty inconvenient. Who has time to build a friendship from scratch whenever they need a tomato, or a permit to sell tomatoes? Buying friendship can seem more convenient than courting and winning it. But in your personal life, you know better than to buy friendship. When business mixes with personal life, the same wisdom should hold.

To create friendship with a government buyer or regulator, the fundamental things apply. Take time to learn about his country and his life. He does not think of himself as a cog in a bureaucratic machine; he thinks of himself as someone you'd like to get to know. Give him the chance to learn about you and your life as well. Friendship can lead to corruption; but corruption cannot be eliminated by eliminating friendship.

Teaching your friend about your life is as important as learning about his. He may perceive you to have unlimited riches. You probably do not feel that you have unlimited riches. This needs explaining. Not the fact that your kid's braces cost more than their average annual wage. But the budgets and reports and objectives and ratios and assessments that constrain your life. Your world of tight accounting controls and legal liability is not obvious. Your friend might assume you can bribe your way out of corruption charges. Many appropriate anecdotes will be necessary to convey the constrictions you face. If there are similar constraints in the country you're visiting, explore the topic together. You might event call respectful attention to that country's anti-corruption penalties.

Your new friend might try to enlist you in his travel plans. He may want a paid trip to your country, or help getting a visa, or a foreign scholarship for his son. Such requests range from modest to enormous. Your friend may not understand your financial limitations, and if you compare the cost of your visit to his country (plane ticket, hotel, taxis, restaurants) to the local GDP per capita, you can see why. Clarify the magnitude of what is being asked. If your funds are not unlimited, you must communicate that. Explain that all of your firm's funds are committed through specific budgets for specific expenses. No funds are available outside this framework. This is not obvious.

Friendship creates the space to say no and develop an alternative relationship.

In some contexts, a trip to headquarters or a training program in your country is quite reasonable. It focuses the relationship on information. For a relationship that should center on the quality of your product, a tour of your home operations, or a class at your trade association, can reward your foreign counterpart while maintaining focus on the business at hand. Public funding is even available for this sort of executive development.

The information value of bringing someone to tour your world should not be underestimated. Soviet Premiere Nikita Khrushchev visited a General Motors plant in North America in the 1950s. He reportedly insisted that the parking lot was fake, refusing to believe so many factory workers owned cars. Misunderstandings can be identified and resolved through such in-person experience.

Alcohol consumption is central to building rapport and trust in some countries. It may not be optional. In some cultures, alcohol is considered the fast track to honesty. If you do not drink, it's assumed you are hiding something.

You may give gifts in the context of friendship, but they should have a low monetary value and a high thoughtfulness component. These gifts are your appreciation for the individual, with their likes and dislikes, not a form of compensation. A textbook on internal control might make an interesting gift.

The idea of modeling business on friendship is not as warm and fuzzy as it sounds. Behind displays of friendship lies the belief that business is a win-lose activity. Do not assume others hold the American belief that business is a win-win activity. Often, it's assumed that one side gets the better of things. A business proposal is received as an attempt to take advantage of someone.

Take every opportunity to describe your win-win vision, but do not expect others to adopt it quickly.

The friendship road seems risky because the person you are getting to know can still make corrupt overtures and then act offended if denied. But in the end, rejecting a corrupt offer is less damaging than treating a person like a role rather than a friend. Friendship creates the space to say no and develop an alternative relationship. Yes, your friend will be disappointed. They will remind you of their urgent needs. But they will know that you have done the right thing, even if they don't acknowledge it.

There is status attached to operating with integrity. Your associate joins a worldwide network of progress. You can buy them a membership in Transparency International. In appropriate circumstances, you can nominate them for a T. I. Integrity Award. Make them feel good about weaving a fabric of integrity instead of feeling bad about the riches they imagine to have slipped through their grasp.

The personal touch may be expected in brief transactions as well as long term relationships. One encounter at an African airport is etched in my memory. A friend of mine was submitting to a full body search, and the security lady found birth control pills in her purse. "Tu ne veux pas des bébés?" (You don't want babies?), the attendant snapped. My friend reacted with anxiety, fearing to miss her plane if she gave the wrong answer. Chatting about contraception with a security guard is not something one imagines one's self doing. But it could have been just the thing. Years later I grew to understand the pure entertainment value of rifling through an American girl's cosmetic case. The African security guard may have been curious because the girls she knew wanted as many babies as possible. My friend could have taken a moment to exchange views.

As you build personal rapport, your overseas contact may wish to discuss world affairs with you. He may express disapproval of your country's leaders. Do not be defensive. But do not join him in disrespecting your country. While honest self-examination is a virtue, this is likely to be a one-way discussion. Your associate may not be feel free to engage in honest examination of his country. Blaming all frustrated human aspirations on your country is a convenient way for him to vent. Your efforts to be agreeable could lead you to join him in condemning your nation. Expressing disdain for your own culture is not confidence-inspiring. Maintain a healthy level of pride, lest he opt for a competitor who does.

Your associate may try to evoke guilt to his advantage. You must be clear that you are not responsible for the state of the world. Your country is not responsible for the state of the world. Life is not perfect, but living conditions are better, even for the poor, than they have been in human history. Two hundred years ago, no one on earth had electricity, sanitation, or reliable birth control. Every year more people get these things. Progress is not covered in the media. News is defined as crisis. The news is designed to appeal to the human mind, which seeks information on future danger rather than past accomplishment. If news is inherently negative, the more news a country broadcasts, the more negative the country will appear. If TV and movies comprise much of your associate's picture of your country, you must elaborate that picture.

Material limitations have been a fact of life since humans first walked the Earth. This is neither a new crisis nor evidence of wrongdoing on your part. Adults all over the world make choices and are responsible for the consequences of their choices. Yet it is human to vent frustrations at safe outlets rather than real causes. There is no value in volunteering to yourself or your firm for safe venting.

If someone gives you the run-around and invokes your guilt,
remember that he is hurting his own people.

b. Communicate system integrity in detail

If you spend much of your life around abstractions like contracts, budgets, accounting principles, and government regulations, they feel very real to you. Your sense of obligation toward abstract conventions may not be shared by your associates. They may reserve their sense of responsibility for the inter-personal sphere and not the legal sphere.

When all of life is viewed as an exchange of personal favors, legal favors may not be sharply distinguished from illegal favors. If you want contracts, budgets, accounting principles, government regulations and internal procedures to be honored, you must make on-going efforts to communicate that.

This approach was used to great success by the government of Hong Kong. Before the 1970s, Hong Kong was so corrupt that when firemen showed up at a fire, cash would change hands before the firemen pointed their hoses in one direction or another. If you grew up there, that's how you saw things get done. In the mid-70s, an agency called the Independent Commission Against Corruption was created. One of its many successful programs was an effort to teach people, including schoolchildren, what services they are entitled to without cash payment. They were told that they do not have to pay the garbageman to pick up their trash or the mailman for their mail. Other successful efforts were anti-corruption television commercials and a television series about detectives investigating corruption crimes.

The underlying strategy is simple: if you want a process to work according to the rules, make sure the rules are public. Do not assume the rules are obvious. If you expect business to flow according to regulations, say it. Use every opportunity to describe your expectations about a transparent process, and try to reach agreement about each stage of the workflow *before* proceeding to it.

Make it clear that you are *not* looking for a special service, and therefore you are *not* planning to pay a fee for extra service. You are trying to elucidate the regular service. By way of analogy, you could explain the availability of toilet paper in the free world.

The person you are working with is a manager of something. Appeal to his perspective as a manager. Speak to him as one manager to another. Get information on accountability as it operates in his organization, and build on that.

Don't give up too quickly. If you are told your papers haven't been processed yet, call back. There are stories of people who called back twice a day for a month and succeeded in getting their affairs attended to without a bribe. If you have to pay someone to make the calls for you, it's still cheaper than paying a bribe—and you get more educational value for your money. Of course, if the phones don't work, you need another strategy.

Many countries have a government procurement code—a detailed open-bidding process for government purchasing. Ask for a copy, and attempt to discuss it with your local associates. The Transparency International website provides a model procurement code with detailed rules for fair competitive bidding. Print a copy and refer to it. If your associate protests that this is not the law of his country, he has incentive to produce a copy of his country's law for your reference. Having the law in hand won't lead to instant change. But it will be one step on the long road toward the shared expectation of fair competition.

Explain the internal controls you live with in your home organization. No bad will is intended by these procedures; they are simply the facts of life in modern organizations

Budgets and auditing are a routine part of system integrity. Accounting scandals only prompt headlines where they are exceptions to the rule—where respect for budgets, audits, accounting principles, and documentation of resource flows is the norm. In places where rules of financial disclosure and fiduciary trust are only acknowledged by a wink in the breech, accounting scandals are not "news." The norm is that people with access to resources spend them however they want, and no one comes investigating.

Explain the internal controls you live with in your home organization. Describe the financial controls you expect in your local venture. Perhaps you expect all expenditures to be planned, documented, consistent with the agreed set of accounting principles, and reviewed through internal and external audits. No bad will is intended by these procedures; they are simply the facts of life in modern organizations worldwide. Do not assume this is obvious.

If you are interacting with an organization whose written rules are unavailable or too vague, pursue a verbal understanding of applicable regulations and the enforcement process. Instead of advocating for "your way," be prepared with information about an effective process in relevant third countries or international organizations. Suggest putting any shared understandings in writing; and propose a public posting of this working agreement. Treating everyone by the same rules is a concept that may not be on the agenda, and no one may appreciate you for putting it there, but it's a worthy goal.

Sometimes the law is so vague that neither party knows whether a law has or been broken or not.

Bringing other parties into the process can be helpful. Gather information on other decision makers relevant to your business, and see if agreements can be extended to them. Exercise caution by gathering information on local rivalries in the public and private sector.

Your competitors are significant others. Creating an "integrity pact" with your competitors is an innovative strategy. Transparency International champions this "islands of integrity" approach. Regardless of how things are handled in the rest of the country, a special agreement on your project can be reached among all bidders and procurement officials. The pact members watching each other will enforce it in the absence of government efforts.

Acknowledge any cooperation you get from your local associates. In their view, your insistence on written rules is indeed asking for special treatment. You may be costing them "face" as well as material benefit. Reward their embrace of due process with expressions of respect and goodwill for them, their organization, and their country.

c. Negotiate

In many countries, drivers are stopped by policemen seeking cash. Locals often respond by negotiating down the amount, without directly acknowledging the true nature of the transaction. Which law the driver broke is not always clear. In some cases, the driver knows exactly what he did wrong—perhaps taking the law lightly because he can buy his way out of trouble. In other cases, no law was broken—the policeman just perceives revenue-generating potential. And some of the time, the law is so vague that neither party knows whether a law has or been broken or not. The rules of the road are just one negotiating point in deciding what it will cost you to get on your way.

Prices are generally fixed in the United States, and most Americans have not bargained except for their cars. In other parts of the world, people are in the habit of negotiating the price of almost everything they buy. Your local associate may feel quite comfortable about negotiating special arrangements. Indeed, they make take pride in their negotiating skill and look for opportunities to exercise it.

Imagine walking into an American auto dealer and saying, "I don't want to haggle. Just give me your best price." They might say okay, but you should not just assume that you've gotten their best price. Probably they expect you to haggle anyway, so they have built in some maneuvering room. Long-held expectations do not instantaneously change at your suggestion.

Corruption can work this way. Anything asked of you should be considered an "opening offer" rather than the "best offer." The word "offer" here is used loosely since it may be a regulation or a time frame rather than an amount of money you are bargaining over. If you are told it will take one month to process your papers, they may expect you to say, "I can't wait one month. I need it in one week." And then you will agree on two weeks; although it may not actually happen for two months.

Or perhaps a regulator insists on inspecting 100% of your shipment. They might expect you to propose sampling 2% of the shipment, and to bargain from there. Bargaining over the substance of a regulation could be the local routine.

Negotiating experts are often brought in to help. If your car is stopped by police, your chauffeur (a widespread institution in low-wage countries) does the negotiating. When you enter a foreign economy, you often choose a partner who's accomplished in local bargaining. This does not completely eliminate the problem because you now have to negotiate with him. Find out as much as possible about your local allies and avoid those whose only credential is that they are "well-connected." Connections without production is a red flag for corrupt practices.

A trade-off between time and money is inevitable. You probably have heavy deadline pressure, but for the person on the other side of the table, dickering with you may be his biggest opportunity. If you are firm and clear, he may conclude that his time would be better spent dickering with someone else. He may even be glad to hand your dead-beat case off to someone else.

Time is money, but time spent fighting corruption can save more money than it costs. Locals spend time shopping for the best clerk or regulator to transact with. In some places, people travel across town to for the best place pay their electricity bill. (In the worst case, you have to tip the clerk or they will they pocket your payment instead of marking your account "paid." Paying bills by mailing checks is not an option in most countries.) Hi-tech solutions to integrity problems should be explored. Debit cards are sold to electricity customers in some countries as a way of assuring that electricity revenues wind up where they need to be. Consumers turn on the power at home with the pre-paid card. The power shuts off when the value on the card is used up.

Negotiations always hinge on what's at stake. In many countries, you have to bribe the coroner's office to get a relative's death certificate. They know you need it for your life insurance claim, so the cash stakes are high. When you have a baby, you have to bribe to get a birth certificate because they know it entitles you to certain benefits. (If you didn't have a baby, perhaps a bigger bribe would get you a birth certificate anyway.) Government clerks sometimes demand a "tip" just to give you the application to apply for a government service. Your bargaining position is weak when everyone knows what you have at stake. If you have built a huge facility in a country, you cannot just take your ball and go home. You are a tempting target for every government official with any conceivable excuse to regulate your facility.

When you have no where else to turn for bargaining chips, you can consider causing legal or political trouble for the person who is extorting you. Gather evidence and bring it to the attention of interested parties from their country or yours. It will not win you friends, but it might weaken enemies. One international manager cited a curious Chinese expression to describe this strategy: "sometimes you have to kill a few chickens to scare the monkey."

The best weapon in negotiations is information. The more you know about past cases and future risks, the less likely you will be to agree to unreasonable demands. Focus discussions on the process rather than final numbers. Ask how the process is managed, speaking one-manger-to-another. Like walking on a high-crime street, look for ways to communicate that you are not an easy target. Display confidence in your integrity, and mention your highly placed friends.

I must communicate these things instead of assuming they're obvious:

☑ I do not have unlimited funds at my disposal

☑ I am constantly being audited and evaluated by my organization

☑ I think business is a win-win activity

☑ I take time to get to know others

☑ I do not think friendship obligates me to satisfy illegal expectations

☑ I believe in integrity regardless of where others stand

☑ I did not cause the world's problems; they have always been there

☑ I am not looking for special services

☑ I want a clear explanation of the regulatory process

☑ I would like a public, written rendering of the rules

☑ I will walk away from unreasonable demands

☑ I give gifts of low cash value that are unique and special

7 Aren't We Really Just as Corrupt?

Yes. **Some of us are tempted into wrongful self-dealing when there's no reliable law enforcement.**

No. **Accountability is built into our system so that large-scale wrongdoing is caught, punished and deterred.**

My story

The lunch counter at my son's school is staffed by parent volunteers. Once a month, I stand in front of a cash box and sell snacks to students at the speed of light. By the time the bell signals the end of lunch, I have a little mountain of cash in front of me. Like the other mothers, I go home and don't think about it until next month.

This cash-management system alarmed one of the mothers. A single staff person counted the cash, deposited the cash, withdrew cash the next day to purchase supplies, and generated monthly financial statements to account for it all. "No system in America runs like that," the mother fumed. The current employee was above suspicion, she thought, but without checks and balances the risk of eventual trouble is huge.

At the time, I thought she was over-reacting. Eventually, I appreciated her point. Even churches have multiple safeguards for managing cash between the collection plate on Sunday and the opening of the bank on Monday. At my father's church, different volunteers count the cash each week. There are always two counters, and they must sign their names to the written total. A third person has the key to the church's safe and witnesses the locking in of the reported amount. Trust, but verify.

Yes.　Some of us are tempted into wrongful self-dealing when there's no reliable law enforcement.

"You're just as corrupt as we are," a Mexican friend once said to me. "You're just richer. If an American road builder wants to steal enough to buy a Mercedes, he takes an inch off each side of the road. If a Mexican contractor wants to buy a Mercedes, he has to steal the whole road."

This logic is wrong. Self-dealing is not justified by putting it in absolute versus percentage terms. Corruption does not stop once the Mercedes is bought. Corrupt individuals continue amassing whatever they can get their hands on— often more than they can spend in one lifetime. They steal to the limits of their access to the public trough.

People are more likely to engage in corrupt behaviors when they believe they can get away with it. Corrupt leaders seize power by force, kill their rivals, jail their critics. In some countries, the main function of government is to seize resources and distribute them to supporters. All resources—foreign aid, taxes, state-owned natural resources (such as oil and gas), and fees for services (i.e. telecommunications, transportation and electricity charges), are sucked up by anyone with the power to do so. The institutions of law enforcement are too weak to resist.

Democratic institutions like elections or a judiciary may exist nominally but are too weak to constrain those in power. Citizens are used to this system. They can either go along or risk severe reprisal. Corruption backed by violence is a stark reality. We disrespect those who live with this terrible burden when we use the word "corruption" metaphorically to equate subtle legal wrangling and personal resentments with real violence-backed corruption.

Wrongful self-dealing, big or small, is a decision calculated on the risk of getting caught. According to research on jurisprudence, enforcement systems work when 80-90% of the people comply voluntarily. When more people break the rules, the enforcement system can't keep up. Voluntary compliers start feeling grieved and go over to the other side. Trust in the institutions of law is the precious foundation of the organizations that meet human needs.

No. Accountability is built into our system, so that large-scale wrongdoing is caught, punished and deterred.

Politics is emotional drama. Disappointments and resentments are inevitable. Your political frustrations are *not* the same as large-scale seizure of public resources backed by brutal violence. If you are convinced that they are, you need a lot more information about the political violence and theft of public resources occurring in the countries at the bottom of Transparency International's Corruption Perception Index. The people who live under such regimes do *not* benefit from equating your experience with theirs. It denies their reality and demeans their suffering. Their only hope is to have what you have: a system of rules. You benefit from living under a system of rules. Why pretend otherwise?

Corruption is often confused with influence. Influence is part of life—human beings are continually influenced by the people they come in contact with. Influence is not corrupt unless there's a lack of accountability.

Imagine, for example, that a beautiful young lady lobbies her president for a piece of land that she's fond of. If the leader uses public funds to buy the land and gives it to her as a gift, that's corrupt. If the leader asks his legislature to turn the land into a national park, it's not the same. The young lady may be fond of the land, but the park is open to the public and administered by the legislature according to the rules established for the national park system. Lobbying is not corrupt when decisions makers are accountable to rules.

Of course, the young lady influenced subjective preferences about which land to turn into a park. There is always room for subjective preferences within the scope of a rule. You may complain that your preferences did not prevail. But that is not the same as corruption. Many people use the word corruption loosely when a leader does not share their perception of a situation. Your leaders cannot be accountable to everyone's personal preferences. They are accountable to the established rules of the system. In truth, you cannot even be sure what your personal preferences would be if you were actually steering the ship rather than just complaining about the steering. If you had all the facts, you might have chosen that same land for a park, too.

Accountability separates functional systems from dysfunctional systems. A village where you can chop wood from the bridge to make your fire is not a place one would choose to build a wooden bridge. Yet that may be the village most in need of a bridge. The best way for the village to get itself a bridge is to create a system that catches and punishes wood-stealing. The system would have to apply to everyone, even the village chief and his friends and relatives. Then it would prevent the destruction of assets, and protect the creation of new assets.

Searching for firewood is not a problem urban readers can identify with. Searching for parking raises the same system integrity issues. Your parking problem can be solved quickly by parking illegally. But when your car blocks traffic, it makes me late. If there's no system to enforce parking rules, I will be tempted to save time by parking illegally, too. Enforcement is unpleasant at the moment you frantically need a spot. In the long run, though, you are better off in a system that enforces parking rules for everyone.

System integrity is extremely difficult to sustain. To understand how much is involved, consider a simple system for re-stocking toilet paper in a school's bathrooms. First, adequate funds for such supplies must be budgeted, though everyone in the system can think of ways they'd rather spend the money. No school funds can be spent without a purchase order, which can only be issued with a manager's signature. The manager can only approve expenditures authorized by the budget, if he cares about keeping his job. Anyone who doesn't like it can bring it up during next year's budget process.

The company selling the toilet paper only sends a shipment if it receives a purchase order signed by the responsible manager. When a shipment arrives at the school, the truck driver will not unload it until a school employee signs a receipt. The school employee is responsible for verifying that the shipment conforms to the purchase order. The shipment comes with an invoice requesting payment. A different school employee instructs the bank to transfer funds to the toilet paper company after verifying that what is being charged conforms to what was ordered. All expenditures are precisely controlled and documented because a purchase order only authorizes a specific quantity to be purchased from a specific vendor at a specific price.

Inventory is controlled as well as money. Someone is personally accountable for the toilet paper at all times. When a janitor removes toilet paper from the storage area to restock the bathrooms, he reports the quantity and his name on an inventory sheet. When the stock of toilet paper is almost gone, the inventory records trigger another purchase order.

What would happen if the principal of a school decided to cut the toilet paper budget to fund his pet project? If no one dared oppose him, the school bathrooms would have no paper. The children would have to tell their parents, who would have to appeal to authorities, who would have to investigate the principal until the problem is resolved. In some places, this would happen. But in some places, children do not expect the paper and parents do not expect authorities to exert budgetary control over the principal.

Virtually every roll of public toilet paper in the United States has gotten there this way. Almost every employee in the United States expects to be held accountable through such procedures. Most people expect violations to be caught because procedures are monitored at many levels. Discrepancies are reported and investigated, and when corroborated by evidence result in lost jobs and disgrace. No one is above the law—school officials are controlled by budgets and audits and investigations and penalties like everyone else. If you hear news about a school official punished for stealing funds, it shows that the system is working. If everybody did it, it would not be news, and it would not be punished. The news reminds everyone that it's foolish to take such risks. No one can misappropriate resources and expect to get away with it for long.

Accounting controls link every organization to every other. For example, the school budget comes from the government, which only releases funds to the school by making deposits into a specific bank account. The bank only releases the school's funds according to strict procedures. The web of procedures and safeguards encompasses the trucking company and the school's outside auditors. Both the truck drivers and the auditors risk losing their credentials and their income if they violate their procedural responsibilities. If misconduct were suspected, the employee accused would be entitled to a legal defense, and the lawyer's credentials would likewise be part of the procedural web.

Even with all these systems in place, toilet paper can be stolen from the rest room stalls. In the United States, many theft-proof toilet paper containers have been invented and many suppliers actively compete for the public restroom business. Do we buy these containers because we're rich? Or are we rich because we buy these containers? Because we take every precaution to safeguard assets so that people who pay for them get the value intended. In the long run, protections save more money than they cost. Protecting resources creates affluence; failing to protect resources creates poverty.

All of these systems must function for the "free" world to be free. Otherwise, you have to bring your own toilet paper, and your own drinking water, and make your own electricity, and air-freight in reliable products, and send your savings out of the country. In the end, it's cheaper to have a system with integrity.

There will always be people looking for ways to circumvent the safeguards on public resources. Preserving system integrity requires constant effort. Violators must be found and punished, and their methods must be studied to prevent future violations. These efforts sometimes result in public scandals. The news headlines mean the system is working. Self-dealing is deterred by the high likelihood of getting caught and publicly shamed. Washing dirty laundry in public creates a bad impression, but it leaves cleaner laundry.

How to stop toilet paper thieves and others with greasy fingers:

☑ Publicize clear rules about who has access to what resources

☑ Enforce the rules all the time and in more than one way

☑ Punish violations according to standard impersonal rules

8 What Difference Does One Person Make?

a. If not you, who?
b. You have an impact, but it's not visible in the short run.

My story

One morning in Africa I woke up with strep throat. My room-mate offered to get me a doctor on his way to work. "When the doctor comes, give him this bottle of champagne," he said. But I didn't. I could not bring myself to hand champagne to a doctor.

My friend was furious when he found out. He was a Belgian with lots of Third World experience. From his perspective, tak-ing a favor from the doctor without returning a favor is rude, not to mention hurts his ability to get future favors from the doctor. A student raised in Poland told me, "Bringing a chicken to the doctor was just common courtesy, or a basket of eggs if you couldn't afford a chicken." In China, patients bring a "red enve-lope" full of money for the doctor when they are admitted to the hospital. A doctor who refused the gift would likely cause the patient to fear for their health.

But there's more to the story. The "free" public health service in Third World countries often employs doctors with friends in the government. They are not accountable for working any par-ticular number of hours. They can spend their days seeing pri-vate patients while lines at public clinics stretch around the block.

The champagne in question was worth more than one month of the doctor's salary at local retail prices. (We had duty-free access.) If you think the doctor's low salary justifies such bar-ter, you should know that bus fare to the clinic cost patients a huge percent of their income. Some walked for hours with sick and dying children. Some will wait on line all day, overnight, and the next day, while their children catch each other's diseases.

When patients get prescriptions from the doctor, they have to purchase their "free" medicines, even when the drugs were donated to the country. Patients admitted to a hospital must supply their own sheets, food, even IVs—the rack as well as the bags of medicine. A student from Africa told me these supplies get stolen from sleeping patients by hospital staff, and sold to other patients. My student tried to donate medical supplies to his own country and couldn't get a permit to ship them without making a payoff. Finally, he went to the Minister of Health in person, and the secretary would not let him in without a payoff. He refused, and the country lost the medicine.

For years, I debated the bottle of champagne in my head. Was I insensitive? Then I got a new piece of information. Transparency International initiated a "Bribe Payers Index," and Belgium was the top-ranking country for offering as opposed to receiving bribes. Perhaps my Belgian friend was a little too quick to offer rewards that violate system integrity?

When you're really sick, you do what you must to survive. But if we feel entitled to survive by breaking the rules, we can convince ourselves that every whim is survival—even champagne. Soon, the rules are broken so often that chaos threatens everyone's survival. A vicious cycle of more rule violations and more chaos can result.

Virtuous cycles are also possible. One of my students visited an African health clinic while she was home visiting her parents. Her eyes itched, and her mother insisted she see a doctor. She waited on line and when it was her turn, the doctor was someone who knew her. "You should have come straight to me," he said. "Why did you wait on line?" She looked around and saw people with bleeding head injuries. "I wasn't my turn," she answered. "You've become so American," he said with disdain. My student came from a poor family. Did she follow the rules because she succeeded? Or did she succeed because she follows the rules?

a. If not you, who?

Maybe you want other people to change first. Maybe you want the government to do it.

You cannot control what others do. Your own choices are the only thing you control, so you might as well use them wisely. If everyone waited for someone else, nothing would ever change.

Waiting for the government is an excuse for inaction. Why should the government change in a country where everyone accepts corruption as the norm? History shows corrupt governments often replaced by new corrupt governments, even when anti-corruption platforms brought the new leaders to power. Honest leaders have difficulty changing corrupt systems. Changing the head does not automatically change the whole body, as anyone who has tried to give up smoking or over-eating knows well. Stopping corruption is like stopping any bad habit—no quick fixes can substitute for daily follow-through.

It sounds like a cliché to say that if you're not part of the solution, you're part of the problem. But every religion and philosophical tradition has a teaching about the significance of individual action. Perhaps the best summary is the story about the boy throwing starfish stranded on the beach back into the ocean. An observer asks him: "What difference can you make? You can never throw them all back." Picking up a starfish and tossing it to the water, the boy answers, "I made a difference to that one."

You make a difference every time you respect rules, because you contribute to the perception of a rules-based world.

"Never doubt that a few committed people can change the world," said anthropologist Margaret Mead. "Indeed, it's the only thing that ever has."

b. You have an impact, but it's not visible in the short run.

Things change, but not in ways that are immediately visible. A hundred years ago, child labor was the norm. Now headlines about child labor shock us because it's the exception. In years past, open sewers and domestic violence were accepted and overlooked. Now we have the luxury of noticing them with horror and working to change them. The more these problems are solved around the world, the more agitated we are by each instance, so we don't notice the progress.

Making accusations of corruption would land you in jail or executed in most of the world just two decades ago. Today, things have improved to the point that we are free to notice and act on such problems. That should be gratifying; we must not let ourselves be discouraged by expecting the world to be perfect instantly.

A great example of successful change is fire safety. Many people burned to death in years past. Today, fire deaths are rare; even huge fires kill relatively few people. How did we get from there to here? With colossal effort. Think of all the fire regulations you encounter in your life. Think of how these regulations are enforced. Many people get annoyed by fire-safety rules, and one never knows which specific prevention effort actually prevented a fire. It's easy to criticize the regulations when you live in a world safe from fire deaths, and overlook how it got that way. Some people even evade the rules and then make accusations when a fire occurs.

Historical change results from a huge number of small efforts. We tend to under weigh progress because as soon as one problem is solved, our minds shift to the next problem. System integrity has made huge strides over the past centuries in the wealthier parts of the world, thanks to colossal efforts in record-keeping, rule-making and enforcement. Now it is time for the rest of the world to enjoy the rewards of a rules-based system.

Recommended Reading

Bribes: The Intellectual History of a Moral Idea by John Noonan

Corrupt Cities by Robert Klitgaard

Fighting the Mafia by Leoluca Orlando (Mayor of Palermo, Sicily)

The Government Inspector by Nikolai Gogol (a play set in
      19th-century Russia)

The Moral Basis of a Backward Society
      by Edward Banfield (Southern Italy in the 1950s)

No Longer At Ease (a novel set in Nigeria)
      by Chinua Achebe, Nobel Laureate in Literature

Tropical Gangsters by Robert Klitgaard

Trust by Francis Fukuyama

Center for International Private Enterprise [*www.cipe.org*]

Transparency International [*www.transparency.org*]

How do you thrive without bribes?

Please send me your story.

LBreuning@SystemIntegrityPress.com

Read other people's stories at www.SystemIntegrityPress.com

About the Author

Only one generation separates me from the life of hardship described in this book. My grandfather was born in Sicily, Italy. The Mafia was not our culture. I didn't even know about it until I grew up and went to the movies. And yet, it was real. Public resources disappeared into private pockets. Honest business was scared away. Most of the harm was done to our own people. Yet individuals have stood up for system integrity, some at great personal cost. I honor their example.

The rule of law shaped my life in another way. Child labor is the norm for peasant families, and school is considered a luxury. One observer in the early-twentieth century reported that every Italian child beyond toddling brought in more money than it cost his parents to feed him. My parents went to school because America has compulsory schooling laws, and the laws are enforced. I honor the system that allowed me to graduate from Cornell and Tufts Universities and become a Professor of International Business at California State University, Hayward.

My father owned a small shop when I was growing up. Mom-and-pop shops were declining even then, and I often saw my father standing around waiting for business. I think of him when I see women selling piles of mangoes with tiny children beside them. These children sit still in a way my children never would. Low productivity systems seem draining, spiritually and materially. Why don't they put all the manoes in one pile so all the other women and children can go home?

"You don't understand the culture," people have told me. "It's a social thing. Each lady sells to the people who know her."

Then I read an interview with market ladies in "Tropical Gangsters" by Robert Klitgaard, a pioneer of corruption research. Each lady rode an all-night bus to bring her harvest to market. She'd stay at the market until everything sold, typically four days and nights. The expense of this trip ate up half of each woman's earnings. Why didn't they organize, so only one woman from the village had to make the trip? They told him they wouldn't trust anyone to bring home their fair share of the money.

Trust and organization are central to modern living standards. Trust is not an emotion; it's the expectation of an outcome. If I give you my assets to invest, I trust that our agreement will be honored—by you or by some back-up enforcement system. It's not perfect, but it works often enough for huge projects to get built. These projects and organizations enhance my quality of life and I do not take them for granted.

Many students have honored me with their personal stories. Most of my students are immigrants or children of immigrants from Asia, Latin America, Africa or the post-communist bloc. Their experiences with bargaining, corruption, and integrity have taught me a lot.

I learned from Elias Garcia's determination to do business honestly in Mexico. Elias finished high school despite having to choose between lunch and bus fare home each day, since he didn't have money for both. He moved to California, but decided to help his family by starting a business for them back in Mexico. A man in their province was known for his business ethics, and Elias decided to be like him. When I was setting up my business, complying with one regulation after another after another, I thought, "if Elias could do this in Mexico, I can do it in California." Yet in the end, Elias had to cut ties with the business he started. His major supplier refused to keep legal accounting records. That made Elias responsible for the supplier's taxes under Mexico's Value-Added Tax system.

Many of my students learned to bribe from their parents. They saw parents pull out cash when transacting with authorities, and even had cash given them by parents with instructions on how to hand it over. But parents also taught them how to resist corruption. Ashok Choudhury left India for Nigeria, where his father worked for an international organization. When his father learned that kickbacks were part of the routine, he quit the job and brought his family home. Now, Ashok accepts having to walk away from a deal some times to avoid compromising his integrity. Like Elias, he knows he's part of the solution rather than part of the problem, and that's better than being rich.

In some places, you have to bribe to get your driver's license. Brooklyn, New York was once such a place. In 1937, my friend Emily Stoper's mother went to take her driving test with a $5 bill that her Polish-born father told her to give the examiner. (Think $100 today.) She didn't give the money because, "I knew I was a good driver." And she passed the test. Emily's mother broke the chain. She could have said, "Why should I learn the driving rules when I'll have to bribe anyway." But she didn't. That improved her children's lives, and their children's.

How do you thrive without bribes?

Please send me your story.

LBreuning@SystemIntegrityPress.com

Forthcoming Books from System Integrity Press

Know Your Third World Partner
When prices are not fixed, and private contracts are not enforced, a unique set of skills comes into play. You need to know them.

None Dare Call It Cheating
Why students cheat. Why they get away with it.

Life in the Middle Lane
Everyone knows the problems of the fast lane and the slow lane, but staying the middle lane quite hard. Here's a guide to avoiding the extremes.

So You Married a Rocket Scientist
Are people just flawed equations?

Greaseless
Spanish, French, audiotape and e-book editions.

Check our website for availability
and for more information about Greaseless

www.SystemIntegrityPress.com
greaseless@SystemIntegrityPress.com

Have fun and build skills with

Grease·le$$
the card game

Negotiate billion dollar global investments
with your friends and family.